ed and mabel go to the moon

ed and mabel
go to the moon

Aaron Bushkowsky

oolichan books
Lantzville, British Columbia, Canada
1994

Publication of this book has been financially assisted by the Canada Council

Canadian Cataloguing in Publication Data

Bushkowsky, Aaron, 1957-
    Ed and Mabel go to the moon

Poems.
ISBN 0-88982-137-2

  I. Title.
PS8553.U83E3 1994   C811'.54   C94-910240-7
PR9199.3.B87E3 1994

Published by
OOLICHAN BOOKS
P.O. Box 10
Lantzville, B.C. CANADA V0R 2H0

Printed in Canada by
Hignell Printing Limited
Winnipeg, Manitoba

for katey
who knew
with love

Acknowledgements

Some of these poems have appeared in the following publications: *The Antigonish Review*, *Conspiracy Northwest*, *The Dinosaur Review*, *Fiddlehead*, *Grain*, and *The Malahat Review*.

A special thank you to Barbara Klunder for the cover art and Kris Klaasen for cover design assistance.

contents

ed and mabel go to the moon

low in the smoky blue sky
this silver time
piece that passes
all understanding
is one huge sigh
for mabel

lookit how it sits
on its edge belly up
to the stars   ed says
lookit lookit
belly up and believe

and mabel wants
with every aching part of her being
to take ed's hand
follow him across the lunar
fields of broken stubble
to the ends of the world
where forest green waves
yawn into azure   the colour of the ring
on her second finger   curl into mauve sand
the colour of her cousin's cadillac
wash over feet   two pairs
pink as salmon

delicate she

walks with the wheat
her bare feet quick

across the field's murmur
speckled moon a harvest

of light   across this crop
and that next

section   carried delicate
by wind   not quite a breeze

of sleep   serpentine
hiss of nightgown
                        brushes soundly
through barley now   and beyond

                        sssshhhh
goes so slow

the way you'd imagine
it should   ghostly white

ed frozen
at the edge

of this sibilate vision
behind a barb

-ed wire fence

dusk or dawn

orange splendour
diffuse   directional
collects dust
adds a haze
to colour
a hundred hundred fields
hung in mid air
filters sun to hue
this orange which isn't red
                    or gold
the solitary house
warms to the task
of basking
                window flares
                roof twinkles
                sandpaper eyes
                chimney teeth

all fade in the air/silt
as the sun sinks
     and sinks
and sinks

sunday cat

the cat mabel loves
refuses ed's lap
instead prefers
to wrap around
mabel's neck
as she sits
to knit
on the porch

mabel tells her
stories of the coast
the shanty where
she was born
of days of rain
fogged in for good
of waves growling
like german shepherds
hazy clouds
as low as
the ground making
the long grass slick
as a swamp   puddles
in the garden becoming one

purring like the tractor
tail directing the breeze
mabel's cat yawns

licks white paws then
tries mabel's ear
tongue dry
as gravel

sun fixed
in her feral eyes

time for tea

warm as wind   tea
cup in hand cradled
fingers interlocking   thoughts
dry   wheat working them
back and forth back and

fourth week without rain
without even a trace   the brown
garden   the backs of cows
the same colour   the barn
his own face   stubble
of wheat four inches high
brown as brown can be
                          the tea
ed can almost taste
above the dust
                 clouds/cows
swollen udders
ready to burst   them cows
plodding to the blistered barn
bumping   rubbing sides   bellowing
a storm of trouble

                    ed turns
the handle to the sun
cup rimmed with
                    daisies
hundreds of them and cows
all around   the smell
perfect smell of fresh
paint on the barn   milk
white house beside green willows
and grass so deep
                    almost blue
rain surrounding the house
                    the saucer
in his other hand
now under the cup
                    perfect fit
ed smiles   perfect
spits at the sky
in the tea

memory lane

eroding road becomes field
and vice versa   the field now
leads to nowhere
                        ed walks
the road home
does it slow

head down
hands swallowed in pockets
thinks about the sun
and the way it works with the wind
much harder than he could
much harder than a thousand cultivators
combined   turning the soil over and over

ed's thought this for 13 years

every morning on his way
down the lane to get the mail   and then
all the way back again

it's late august now
and the new sears catalogue is due

dew drop inn was their honeymoon place
just across the american border
26 years ago and mabel still talks
about the prices

ed thinks everything over
      the rising cost of fuel versus
      the dropping price of grain

and does it really matter
where he walks

on the wheat with his leather boots gathering dust
or the other way around zigzagging on and off the lane   the field
the lane   the field   a thousand cultivators
a roaring in his head   this morning
piled on top of every other morning
on top of everything else
coming back empty-handed

stalled

in the half-ton
they watch themselves
reflect in the black glass
ed avoids the obvious
question   what mabel really thinks

the evening spreads itself thin
in sunset's orange trim

from a distance
the barn
is a red thicket fence
stubby moon pales
ed and mabel

road blacked out
by the absence of headlights
as thoughts steam up windows
mabel notices that
they have stalled
in the wrong place

darkening roads
with fields
remain as always

they breathe the night in
breathe out from each other

watch themselves fade

taken up

fields dust their feet

ed and mabel walk
across the outstretched arms
of land   the wind
is there as usual
picks up the dust   and swirls
it into their faces
                    mabel stops
to empty her shoe   her eyes
are blue   the same as sky

they follow ed as he walks away
on waves
          farther and farther
floats to the fence
          and over it
into the light

ed never looks back

mabel's eyes are blue
her dress is white

dirt marks the lines along her palms

she blinks

holds her shoe
to block the sun

mabel brushes her hair

mabel sees herself again
for the first time   the looking
glass look   the fairest
fields of grey   she dips the hairbrush
in water   in the coffee cup
brushes those fields down her shoulder
her back   stroke after stroke

                outside ed passes
                the open window
                sounds of tractor cultivating
                dust   every fourteen minutes
                in the window's frame

the clock in the hallway
counts the hair that doesn't grow
as it should   falling
across her tiny tiny bottles of
perfume   caught in the mirror's
tension   a lined face   and spots
on her hand   seeds in her eyes
a breeze at her mouth   dry and hot

a field of lines

where do the lines end
what is written   the beginning
word which is the beginning

                    ed doesn't believe the good word
                    works sunday as any other day
                    seven a.m. and already two hours
                    on the swather   the field
                    slowly gathers definition
                    concentric rows of wheat   neatly twined
                    patterns   a plain that curves
                    ever so slightly   with the earth
                    away from the eye   the clatter
                    churning wheel behind the rise

where does it begin
to come round   the swather behind the last dip   a sound
you can't visualize   or can
from the wheat falling
together under the blade

                    ed at the wheel knows where he is
                    what time it is   how many laps
                    he's gone   which way the wind blows
                    just by looking behind   the dust
                    of the swather   drifts west
                    toward the highway   where cars head
                    for the baptist church   ed doesn't wave
                    keeps his mind on keeping a perfect line

imagine a field of lines   or better
still   fields of lines as far as you
can see   what patterns cross
the outstretched mind

ed looks at his face in the mirror
unshaven   looks beyond that
sees the sky   a glancing blaze
ed corners sharp on three wheels
counterclockwise   cuts another
line from the perfect field
on the way to the middle

edison

in the late evening
a promise of rain

damp sent swirling across
the barley through the fence
and into the garden

the motorola's ecstatic
lightning seen near lethbridge   calgary
streets running neon through puddles
mabel dreams of fresh salad
mounds of lettuce celery tomatoes
almost beside herself   she finally
takes a deep breath   ed's voice
coming back to life   maybe i
should fly a kite   draw
the lightning over to the back
quarter-section   let it chase me
over to joe's corn   bill's wheat
i could even hook it up to the back
of the half-ton   drive to medicine hat
up to hanna   saskatoon   jeezus i could even
get on the national   cbc could do a big special and
then a rumble knocks the tv dead

ed and mabel look
at each other

thunder-burst laughs
until they cry

ed's nose ripening

that paper gull

white on white/blue
so low on mabel's mind

the letters in the sock
drawer   vancouver

island   cool and
pure   imagined

sand   long beach
of surf

the white sheets of foam
what her mother wrote

about the land
of rain   forests

behind the house
along the shore

sure flat rocks
you could skip across

days mabel sets her mind to
that lone gull   west

behind the red barn
the white snippet

folds and unfolds
high above the sheaves

of wheat   ed's tractor
slow   the way it drags

and drags itself
home

smiles and smiles

ed   as he rides and rides
the field a flat ferris wheel
another turn   another swath
clover up to your heart
falling in perfect perfect rows

ed squints over the photo taped
to the swather window

mabel smiles back from a time
caught twenty years ago in the quick
click   camera's light reminder
of the way things used to be

> mabel with her favourite straw hat
> a blouse her mother made
> buttoned right to the neck
> black boots under the grey skirt
> painful to wear
> all wrong for her feet
> in her gloved right hand
> a folded umbrella
> behind her the sky is all
> so grey

ed turns the wheel
heads for the next row
smiles a swathing smile

it's mabel's eyes
that always get him

perfectly caught in the middle
of a perfect blink

she prays river

to come in her hour of need
from behind clouds
across the quieting wheat
beyond the bright full moon
into the garden   finally to seep
under curtains into the bedroom
where mabel stares at ed caught
in his world of sleep

                    a river   a river   a river

alive with blues and greens
flashing clean and catching stars
she prays

                    a river   a river   a river

eyes tight as if she could see
the land change overnight
water cascading over the flat spaces
down the dusty road
swallowing the barbs   fence after fence
eddies forming around telephone poles
the old red barn finally
                              floating out to sea

mirage

in slow curves   blue
wavers over the edge
floods ed's eyes

that placid space baked in waves
sets what's known to image
airy water   the mirage ranges
rearranges   floats softly
across pastures   sets one picture
swimming after another
              ed's wonder in a
controlled blink
the phantom pain of the prairie
the missing sea   ed's eyes
with the salt stinging
go back to the job at hand
he picks up a bale
throws it on the wagon
behind   the murmur of surf
he doesn't hear

midnight express

mabel's pinkish hands
are in the dirty dishwater
cleaning up again after ed
who sits in the next room
looking out the window
at nothing in particular
waiting for mabel
to finally come to bed

mabel can't sleep when it's so light
she flitters away time
washing dust from the dishes

        click-clack
            click-clack

one dish after another
stacked and restacked
with old newspaper in between

hours and hours until the task
sounds like a dozen things to ed
dozing in the master bedroom
dreams shape sound into a long white table
straddling railway tracks
mabel at one end
ed staring from behind a newspaper
at the other
hundreds of dishes gleaming between them
and then
        then out of the clear blue
a faint whistle and that all too familiar
        click-clack   click-clack
ed can't deny

the call

pale yellow moon
like a sick dandelion
slides between thinning clouds
settles on mabel nesting
in the bed's meadow of
quilts   blankets   sheets

her breath in the fuzzy
world of sleep quickens
a boy calls from
the top of a hill

mabel climbs after him
cement feet straining against
the changing terrain
inside her head
the whole night   one hill after another
this boy she can't recognize
calling her   as faint as dreams allow

this seasonal grace

turns land to frown
lines   the handwriting's
on the wall   ed says
after climbing down
the silo   this year
we'll just watch the paint
dry   ed's voice serious
as usual   scrawls
the living room air

mabel takes her time
listens to him speak his mind
arranges lilacs
on the coffee table   out
side that perfect patch of
horizon and sky   a wall
of dull tones
their conversation
the lilacs between them
ed says he doesn't like
doesn't like the smell   doesn't like
the way they take up the whole room
doesn't like doesn't like doesn't like
the way the purple looks today

as if mabel didn't know
he'd turn too   this season

all grace turns

lullaby for mabel

the beginning
of the end

the way the poem lies
or dies against the sun

picture lines
around the field

fallen wheat
over this hill

and beyond
what the fading

light does
imagine

some wind
then still

come walk with me
whisper what you will

thinking fields

into the kitchen   then
the bedroom   back
again to the kitchen   to
the bathroom   over
to the bedroom   again
the shuffle-shuffle of slippers
mabel with her particular plod
this room and that   hallway stretching into
flowersflowersflowers
all the way to the kitchen
where the wallpaper is
roads   fences   section
after section   down the wall
onto the grey shelf beside the sink
where three silver cups sit
in the sunlight coming through
                        the open window
mabel decides they stand
at the edge
of their property
silos in the morning light
waiting for ed
to run his hand through
scatter a little
gold to the wind

fool's gold

sun panhandles ed all day
finally draws a bronze line across
his arms   his forehead   his neck

in the east section dry creek bed
each breeze flakes gold
'hoppers wave to wave
on wild oats

dust's last visible twinkle caught
on the backs of their bent legs

every step of the way
ed stares as the sun
sets gold-fire to the barn's glass
windows   all seven in a row

at the house

ed empties dust and 'hoppers
from boots and pockets

yellow gold

the small pyramid
disappears overnight

dry clouds and begonias

when a man says he's dead tired
you almost have to believe him
ed's mother wheezed three days before

men men men and their dirty little habits
they spit in the sink   underwear all over the place
reeking of the barn cow shit on their nice wool socks

and no one is more surprised when a strange dog
finds her out behind the house under the clothes line
on the green green grass still wet with dew   two
clothespins in her mouth   ed's longjohns flapping
flags in the wind   white socks dotting the lawn

and no one especially mabel can understand
a woman like that   even at the wednesday afternoon funeral
followed by coffee and cake beside the garden that won't grow
farmers beet-faced in too tight shirts   polishing off
lemonade   keeping their speeches about clouds to three sentences
or less while the women eye the begonias   and mabel
sits in a blue lawn chair fanning herself another vision
children playing tag across wheat over their heads
cutting paths to hills   trees   rain forests
mabel listens to what the people say to ed
and then ed   dead tired from trying to talk
about the weather   dead on his feet from rushing down

the lane and back all week checking on the mail
bills bills bills and maybe a note from his father
who left him high and dry and holding the bag

a dry farm   dry eyes   dry wind
pushing dry clouds away behind the baptist church   clouds
touching each other in tiny perfect rumbles
and everyone hushes
and then ed stares at the clouds
in his shoes

pearls

mabel sits across the mirror
watches herself
the clock behind her
reversed   the picture too
mabel and ed facing the wrong way

mabel remembers the time ed held
pearls in his huge cracked hands
a river of moon   even his smile
had a touch of white

mabel smiles   holds them up
the way she did twenty-five thirty years ago
the night on the porch after rain
when the wind was wet

finally mabel decides they don't match
anything   all the clothes
pressed flowers across two closets
shuffle when the wind scoots through
the room
                    sends a shiver
down mabel's loose naked body
as she sits in the mirror
with the pearls' pale noose
around her sun-lashed neck

dixie

a flower blooming on the side
of her head   ed says the words
over sweet tea   mabel still sobbing
those sobs at the back end of a good cry
little shudders like the last car on a long train
when the whole thing stops empty outside
the co-op granaries   that's the way mabel cries
ed decides   and then goes on
and on saying dixie tried to shake it off almost got up
god-damn it   had to fire two more rounds
into the back of her head   under the mane   right
under the ear   took me twenty minutes to shovel
her under   lime and all   lime spilling like god-damn
sugar   can you imagine   can you
ed says watching mabel rearrange things
above the sink   finally gives up and walks away
across the yard to get the bottle he hides in the barn
mabel at the kitchen window trying to look away
the dog waiting under the steps
without a sound

prairie atheists

sunday morning   dry as hell
can't even see the sun
wind worshipping the ground
sends it to air
by noon the fields are floating
ghosts of themselves

ed says
          living out here
          could make an atheist
          of the pope

says that in a low monotone
a chorus with the wind
falling   a barely raised choir
sound   a hesitant resonance
almost nasal   adrift dusty moans
                            uh
          the kind of sound
          you'd expect from old farmers
          falling asleep in church

ed imagines
               thinly
across psalter hymnals
a fine layer
frosting stained glass
lacing pews   the oak pulpit
the upright piano with the missing keys
salt from the dead sea

dervish in the garden

i

third dust devil today
starts in the east
gathers up its skirt
twists toward the house   soil caught
in the visible vortex
hail tap dances across
arthritic peas   cabbage aghast
carrots shuffle   beans recoil
around bending poles   a newspaper hugs
the edge of a wire fence

mabel watches her world bristle
wonders where they come from
day after day all summer long
these devilish funnels
that waltz back and forth
having devilish fun

wonders if tonight
her garden
will get the last dance

ii

polite rows of starlings
neatly attired sit
on the telephone wires
sway to the gentle sounds
of another dervish dancing through the dirt
through the smoke of burning stubble
around and around the house ed's father built
around and around the orange shed banging broken doors
like giant wooden cymbals around and around
mabel picking up starched clothes
scattered under the wash line   around and around
ed chasing after his hat   around and around and around
while the lights softly go down

said to wind chimes

too much love and wind can drive a man
crazy   ed's words   one right
after another   perfectly rhythmic
a winding down to the single word   right
woman   wrong farm   maybe even the wrong country

this place turns mabel's skin lizard-like
cracks her lips and makes her hair go straight
it's crazy how two people like us tried to make
a go of it ed says   and the men say crazy back

mabel outside blows on a wind chime
the kind with little golden angels in turn
blowing on french horns   ed and his men
roll their cigarettes   watch mabel watch
the angels   watch her purse her lips
wonder what kind of woman
has these angels dancing in her head

raking memories

and after a quiet breakfast with toast and butter
oatmeal porridge to help with the digestion   the screen door
slams   dew is as low as clouds can get ed says
while raking whatever leaves he can find on the brown grass
mabel sitting on a lawn chair nods
reads a book about the coast
and ed wants to touch the back of her neck
wants to run his hand across her shoulders   wants to
kiss her today   wants to run naked with her
across the lawn in the rain   wants to laugh and tell a dirty
joke   wants like anything for everything to be
like it used to   1939 eighteen men on a swathing team
four teams of horses and the women coming from all over
to fix chicken salad sandwiches and there she was
walking toward him carrying butter   bread   a jar
filled with water and three slices of lemon
and the men all stopped
whatever they were doing   saw young ed make
a complete fool of himself doing a jig with this girl
just visiting from the coast   ed's father
watching from the back of the second hay-rack
smoking   as usual   a scowl on his red face

then like now not a cloud in sight
but a different sky

ten grown men reciting poetry
at the central cafe coffee counter

yeah   ain't it a shame
ain't it though
never seen a god-damn
summer like this
that god-damn wind
          pass the fries
that god-damn heat
god-damn cattle droppin
like god-damn flies

the god-damn sky
grey you say
grey my ass
worse   it's grass brown
like chicken eggs
or off-white on a good day
a light white hot
no not hot   muggy
buggy with all those god-damn ticks
and flies and fleas   and jeez
here i'm thinkin it should be
could be

would be
too god-damn hot
for the whole god-damn lot
includin god-damn bugs
                pass the salt
                        please
the worst thing now would be
an early freeze
                thank-you
                        just like last year
or the year before that
flat crops sitting   oh
under two feet of snow maybe more
the way we say stay with it
the good lord's just teasin us
treatin us with patience
with the rain comin down loads
two counties over   with the mountain streams
just burstin at the seams   yeah   so
ain't it a shame
                ain't it though

held patterns

here   by the mind made
ocean   by the mind made
sea

mabel sits on her favourite rock
near her favourite stream in the whole
wide world
                away from the waste
land of dust and dirt   away from ed
and his leathery face   away from his eyes
that look like they belong
in the bottom of a well
                            away from his words
the pattern of
                god-damn this
                    &
                god-damn that

away from his touch
                    his hands
when they make love
                    his hands
burn marks
            on her arms
                        the size of shells

middle-aged

the middle sags
as middles do

    middle of the yard
    middle of the barn
    middle of the afternoon

the list goes on

ed and mabel
on lawn chairs
balancing ice-tea
on their stomachs

the middle of summer
mid-life crisis   rains
on the wrong side
of the mountains

earth
now stretched
to the limit

someone in the middle
of all this says   my
how time flies   of course
the reply   a reply
expected

ed and mabel
lift their glasses

ice in the middle
catches sun
by surprise

bringing in the sheaves

during the six o'clock news
ed and mabel watch the sunset
reflect orange and red
dust on the glass in the line
where mabel ran her finger
a furrow ed studies for a while   he listens
to wind whistle thin through barbed wire
behind the house   down the drive way
the wire scratches the rusty mail-box
he forgot to fix in the spring

mabel reminds him again
during the tide commercial   ed stares
out the kitchen window
glass in hand   he holds the water up
to the sky   eyes brim to the edge
the quarter-section behind the barn
barley barely eight inches high
not enough to sneeze at ed says
to mabel long after the motorola cools

on the porch   mabel brings tea
sits and listens to the wind
then hums   bringing   bringing
in the sheaves   bringing the sounds
into her mind   to feel the sky
and stars and moon sprinkled like dust
while ed holds on to her weathered and spotted hand
the prairie hymn he can't remember

mabel's sunset

i

here the sun
sets for hours

the painting comes later
dusk and the colours run

can't see the wheat then
or ed   he stays out
after the sun
works his way around the fields

there's a pattern to it

yesterday was the same
as last year

ii

once i flew in
saw everything

all the pieces fit

the sun
i thought
            too bright
clouds' shadows
ink spots on a quilt

it was unbelievable
the way things stretched out

even the house
white in the middle of what else
wheat   a lone cloud
sitting on its shadow

iii

i can't imagine
snow   if i could
it would be the same problem
as today

the same things out here
in the dead
of winter
white dust
the way it crowds the window

after a storm
you can imagine

what i mean
the gathering
thoughts of more
to come

iv

i wrote another song
about everything

my life here
the wind

i sang it to ed
he was in the field
as usual

i had to make up
another ending

v

my mother taught me to sing

sitting out on the boat
listening to the waves'
soft pat
turning with wind

sometimes facing the open sea
watching the sun sit
the colours never the same
and the song

all the pieces fit

even now
when i don't know the melody

vi

i wish double
wish i could see
i could really see
everything for the first time

i remember when i first arrived

ed in his best suit
the homestead
the fields
some flowers   purple mainly
those clouds here and there

now when i close
my eyes i know
it's still all
all there

i guess the wish
doesn't really matter

vii

this sunset
four hours

it seems
forever   light

at the edge of the wheat

at the edge of the world

at the edge of the world

wheat with wind dry
with wind dry wheat
wind dry wheat with
dry wheat with wind

ed thinks it over and over
over by the fence
lips dry as the back
of his hands   dry as the sky

thinks it's over
the well's run
dry   wheat with that wind
gets to your eyes   ed says to no one
in particular
                picks at a barb
with a stick
                imagines himself
ploughing it all under
losing more topsoil
                better to leave
it in   ed tells joe
over coffee   every morning
the same subject   wind
taking the top two inches off
to montana
                ed now getting pushed
and pushed as he walks with the wind
the dry dry wind   down the line
to the edge of the world

can't imagine where else
he'd rather be

the same wait

and with the wait
mabel grows tired

the last time it rained
it was tuesday
the tractor didn't work

ed spent the day
waiting for parts

the water pump broke
it would cost forty-nine ninety-nine

the john deere sat
in brittle wheat

there was a seagull
on the seat

it was the only one

you could almost hear
the land sigh

sometimes mabel felt cold
it was the way the sun went

behind it all   the wind
waited too

mabel wore a blue dress
with a grey apron

the dress was twelve years old

you could almost hear
the land sigh

now mabel waits
in the same dress

the day it rained

ed waiting for parts
again the john deere sits with
the lone seagull

the clouds open and close

dusting

the wide open sky
the sheer
fever of fields
around the white house

ed and mabel bake
in the kitchen
where the grey cat
basks under the slow gnaw
of sun   they sit and wait
for the spoken word
the next phrase
heavy across the tiled floor
the way sounds weigh
this day the last day
of summer
or the day after   always
the day after   the same
song wind sells
cracks its high/low
voice against the pane

ed wears his white shirt
with the pearl cuff-links

it must be sunday
or it could have been
mabel's imagination
what she saw
or thought
the look on her husband's face

when he licked his lips
she could hear
the dust move

e i e i o

was the song
someone said over dishes
was the first song
billie learned to sing

when he was seven
he used to pull his wagon
a tractor he said   to
gather eggs   singing as he went
feathers flying like
like a winter storm
              someone says
holding a dish up
to the light

he had them laying like   o
like a factory
old mcdonald would have been proud
he could do anything that boy

ed and mabel later that night
look at photos
                 chickens
                 eggs
                 the old wagon
                 billie

now a lawyer called william
sends money in birthday cards

someone says   it's a good thing
all right   he didn't stay on
the farm   someone says   the city
sure it's the place to be

                    later
in the evening someone
upstairs in billie's old room
at the window   the rosy sun
a warm dish   fading
the old wind
              i e i

              o

the devil himself

today the sun is the same
soaks up the long hot birdless afternoon
filled with flies
       dust
       the absolute
nothingness of dying barley
rows and rows and rows of brown
a graveyard ed says
studies the marks
of the coyote   the devil himself
ed tells mabel over chicken
with mashed potatoes and gravy
digs up the garden   kills the rooster
scares brownie half to death
as if we don't have trouble enough
ed points out with a carrot
then imagines a quick whisper of grey
through the hushed cattails
the sudden chatter of chickens
brownie growls   stares   where the sun strays
into shadows   across the road
another road   in the dying thicket
where the crows never sleep

ed dreams of snow
and that one clean shot

catching things

today
out on the combine
ed's memory works
like this

yeah i'm out fishin with my old man
fishin in the old man river
down the old man road
away from our silver and white trailer
he built from wood he found at the construction
sites and behind the school   yeah we men
me and my old man could do the damnedest things
with absolutely nothin   then
spend the day out doin nothin
away from mother   away from my sisters wearin
them blue yellow and red sweaters
dancin on the shore
this dance that always always stopped
when my old man's boat ground its teeth
into the old man river bank and yeah i was a little man
even back then   nine years old
and castin my hook as fast and as good
as i could   yeah a quick snap of my wrist here and
a quick snap of my wrist there
and sit down in the boat   SIT DOWN
the old man screamin and drinkin   SIT DOWN BASTARD

me just castin my red and white devil out
with a quick regular snap   yeah it's all in the wrists
here and there   castin with my old man   castin out and
across the sky blue water and into the sun
while my little sisters danced around my mother who swayed
and swayed and swayed like a white flower
waitin and a waitin
with a sharp knife to gut the things
yeah we men have caught

whitefish

dreaming mabel
wonders what
it would be like
with a sharper knife
finally decides
on the tomato cutter   the one
that does everything
slides it into
the fish belly
neatly divides
clean across the tender
white underside
and with a quick wrist
off comes the head and
tail   trimmed
and gutted   this fish
is clean as ed's forehead
under his cap
soft as mabel's wrist
under the red sleeve

ed's song

what you have
to do is keep your mind
occupied

every round
every row
every round
every row

let the god-damn swather
do the work

suck on a cherry pit
kills the time
keeps your mouth
from going dry

swat flies
sing a hymn
stand up

sit down again
sometimes i piss off
the side
            one hand does
the job

you do what you have
to do   mind your god-damn work
cut what's left
before the god-damn
wind gets it all

at bay

sometimes absolute
silence creates sound
a ringing of nothing
around the tractor

an ocean of silence
wave after wave

ed is the island
on the john deere
in the uncharted wheat

when he squints
the blur
of home
becomes a ship   mabel
on deck waving
a red towel to come in
or out   the silence
a roar   sand in ed's hair
salt on his lips
       faintly
the held vision
the ship mabel holds to
rides his mind

still ed tries calling
mabelmabel
the grainy voice
lost in the wash

when he turns away
he thinks
she is singing

sound it out

say it   prairie   sound
it out over and over until it sounds
like something else   this is mabel's game today
sitting at the kitchen table   wheatwheatwheatwheatwheat
until a train whistle circles the room   a light shriek
her own making   the way it repeats   landlandlandlandland
as if the john deere won't start   prairie now
strung together as a bird sound   prairieprairieprairieprairieprairie
see   she says to herself over and over   everything
means something different eventually   she says and says
with her hands flat as they can be on the cool table
sometimes you feel it change your mind   pull you
away   a tumbleweed in the sharp sound of wind
roll of words now sounds impossible to place   farmfarmfarmfarmfarm
what is it now she can't decide   the point to it all
where things stop making sense sitting in her warm
kitchen facing the window's idea of sky
the clouds their sound awkward   thick   cloudcloudcloudcloud
caught in her throat   caught sound
and maybe that's what ed meant mabel decides   sometimes
you simply can't break the prairie or catch them clouds
otherwise you'd probably move to the coast
put your feet up and listen
to records

mabel's waltz

a long   long   song
mabel says at the piano

about fences
furrows   rabbits   roads
but mostly fields

the sing
song wind
song   sleepy
sounds
         in tones
drawn to her eyes
fingers slow
walk across
certain and
         uncertain keys

the sky especially
a waltz
cloud notes

the blue
deeper
around the edge

twelve hours

12 a.m.

mabel watches night close in
birds outline the fence
a long winding wind
a cat across loose shingles

mabel leans back on the porch chair
the one she repainted herself
the same colour as her palms
her eyelids   now weighed down
until the dark
fully drawn
clouds over

2 a.m.

mabel wakes
sees her tea cup broken
a tea stain   not tea
but an ink blot   the animals
caught in full flight
those single horns   unicorns pointing to
stars   mabel stares there and there
and there   until it hurts
the moon
          in her half-closed eyes

4 a.m.

she coughs
surprises herself
               trumpets
streaming into her ears
finally slow to crickets
and owl sounds beyond
that thicket
beyond the barn

a long yawn

she is cold
wet arms
morning lawns
hair on end

shivers a bit
more than she expects
pulls the comforter around

counts more crickets
their songs   always
there at night
             she hums
without knowing
they've stopped

6 a.m.

sun moves up
clouds move away
mabel under the patchwork
comforter   her own sky

head low on her shoulder
hair as if combed
                  breath slow
between those ribbons
                     long and
slowing
          morning on her lips
lids so very
            very heavy
catches a little
                 slice of
                              light

8 a.m.

when ed finally finally finds her
he looks and looks   is and isn't surprised
says mabelmabel as if   as if she forgot
and she did   mabelmabel   ed says again   wake wake
up please   but she doesn't move
head low on her shoulder
hair damply sweeping over
rain on the horizon
two drops on her
thin white neck

10 a.m.

ed says she was the god-damn sunshine
of my life and the doctor nods
and nods and nods   thinks
he understands he's sorry
as sorry can be doesn't look
at ed who looks out the window
clicks his god-damn pen

12 p.m.

ed makes sandwiches
for himself
sets the table
for one

wipes the fork
on his shirt

his footsteps
across the floor
a huff shuffle of wind

watches a fly
most the afternoon
caught between the glass
in the kitchen window

no sound

nothin

ed's last lines

i

in 32 we had topsoil
moving like some kind
of god-damn ocean

slow grey waves

you could say
goodbye to your
dream
      the old man said

the way he waved
his god-damn arms

as if he knew

ii

it took us the better part
of the year

that barn
how it still stands
beats me

nothing in it   in fact
nothing to put in it

beams got arthritis bad

wind finds holes
some big enough
to stick your fist through

and so much
god-damn wind

probably the only thing
holding it up

iii

every day
the thing looks thinner

sometimes i think
one good swing
is all it takes

sometimes i want to be
the guy who finally throws it

iv

you know sand blowing
against the house
sounds just like
just like rain   yeah

it fooled me once

still does

especially at night
when i can't find the moon
or wake mabel

v

one good thing for sure
i remember
my mother left pots and pans
strung out by the barn
said the wind and sand
could do a better job
of cleaning

crazy old lady

i can still hear them

but they get further

especially on days
when nothing moves

vi

once we had a dance
in the loft

songs and beer and whisky and everybody
swinging to the sounds   no smoking

unless you went outside
and stood in the rain

i'd take it up
just to do it again

vii

anyway   the god-damn fact is
it's almost finished

thinking about those yesterdays
the first dust bowl
building that old barn
in the heat
waiting for the rain
so we could finally stop

the old man with his beard
full of saw dust

sometimes working till
midnight   then listening
through the unfinished beams
to everything around the farm

everything   every animal he could
name with his eyes closed   and then
predicting the exact day of rain

thing is
we all believed him

the way he said goodbye
to our dreams

the way we built
the god-damn thing up

was some chore
when i think about it